His Sorrowful Passion

Scriptural Chaplets of Divine Mercy

by Christine Haapala

Woodcut Illustrations by Albrecht Dürer

Suffering Servant Scriptorium

Fairfax, Virginia

www.sufferingservant.com

Published with Ecclesiastical Permission
Diocese of Arlington
January 15, 2002

Sacred Scripture verses are from the **Douay-Rheims Bible,** Challoner Version, 1899.

Diary, Saint Maria Faustina Kowalska, Divine Mercy in My Soul copyright © 1987 Congregation of Marians of the Immaculate Conception, Stockbridge, MA 01263. All rights reserved. Used with permission.

The Great Passion series and other woodcut illustrations are taken from the Dover Pictorial Archive Series, The Complete Woodcuts of Albrecht Dürer, copyright © 1963, by Dover Publications, Mineola, New York. These illustrations were originally printed by Albrecht Dürer during the period 1497-1511. The initial drop cap Dürer Gothic Condensed letters are from the Dover Electronic Display Font Collection, copyright © 2000, by Dover Publications, Mineola, New York.

ISBN 0-9703996-3-4; ISBN13: 978-0-9703996-3-2

Kindle version: ISBN 978-0-9840394-4-9

Manufactured in the United States of America.

Dedicated to the
Blessed Virgin Mary, Mother of Mercy, Our Life, Our Sweetness, and Our Hope

Special thanks to Father Michael Duesterhaus for his inspired guidance. In heartfelt gratitude to Father Vincent P. Bork and Nancy Scimone Bash for introducing me to the devotion of the Divine Mercy.

To my family, thank you for all your support and encouragement, especially my husband Ken.

Table of Contents

Publisher's Note: Jesus' spoken words from Sacred Scriptures and quotes from St. Faustina's Diary are bold. This follows the formatting conventions established in the Diary.

Table of Illustrations

Foreword

When topics of justice and mercy arise in conversation, they are put in contrast to each other, as though they were competing forces. This presumption must be faced by any Christian since the Lord God is infinitely just and infinitely merciful and He cannot contradict Himself.

Justice demanded that mankind pay for the Original Sin of pride. Mercy called for the return of mankind to the close embrace of God. Man lacked the ability to reconcile with God and He wanted to respect our freedom that He bestowed upon us. In the life, death, and resurrection of Jesus Christ, justice and mercy are seen in consort: truly God, Jesus had the power to overcome the worst effect of sin, death; truly Man, Jesus freely gave of Himself, to the point of giving His very life.

The Chaplet of Divine Mercy, one of the newest devotions in our ancient Church, guides the believer to a deeper appreciation of the generosity of our Lord. Coupled with quotations from Sacred Scripture, this prayer can be even more integrated into the rich fabric of our Faith.

The intersection of justice and mercy is also found in the life of the Blessed Virgin Mary. The new Eve, free from Original Sin and its effects, Mary saw more clearly than any other person of the condition of mankind and the justice of God's judgment against us. As the new Eve, she was a mother who carried with her a boundless love for her son, Jesus. This is the mother that raised Jesus, who formed him as He grew in His human nature, who reflected to Him the love, tenderness, and mercy of God. Cooperating with the graces provided by God, Mary was able to fulfill the greatest role any person has ever been called to.

St. Michael fighting the Dragon

Jesus said to St. Maria Faustina: **Before I come as the just Judge, I am coming first as the King of Mercy.** *(Diary, 83)*

We, too, are called to cooperate with the graces God provides for us. We are to recall always the salvific death and resurrection of Jesus Christ and see in Him the reconciler of God and Man. Justice and mercy are seen in the eyes of the Christian, not as competing forces, but complimentary ones. Like the two blades of a sword, justice and mercy work toward the same end: cutting us free from sin.

The Gospel demands that all parts of our lives, whether speech or action, thought or deed, reflect the will of God. It is said that this demand is too much for mankind to bear. To such a position we must recall that while much is asked of a Christian, how much more was asked of our Blessed Mother?

Confident in the Blessed Virgin Mary's constant appeal on our behalf in heaven, may our prayer and meditation on the mercy and justice of God be deepened by this chaplet.

Father Michael R. Duesterhaus,
Priest of the Diocese of Arlington, VA

Introduction

Our Lord told St. Maria Faustina: **There is more merit to one hour of meditation on My sorrowful Passion than there is to a whole year of flagellation that draws blood; the contemplation of My painful wounds is of great profit to you, and it brings Me great joy.** *(Diary, 369)*

In your hands you have a guide to spend an hour or any portion of that time meditating on the Passion of Jesus and reap the reward He promised. You also have a guide to ponder Sacred Scriptures and glean untold treasures that were written even before Jesus shed one drop of precious blood. A great understanding of God's love for us flows from the sacred and inspired writers, so that when we dwell on His passion we are never alone. Many who walked before us embraced His wounds with their minds and hearts and shared this immense wealth of their understanding.

Among the writers who have been moved by the Spirit of God to devote their time and talent to assist us in our search to find what God longs for us to know, we have this inspired work of Christine Haapala. Through her prayerful reflection on the sacred word, she challenges us to drink and eat from the vastness that the Spirit offers. We can better grasp the notion that **"Not in bread alone doth man live, but in every word that proceedeth from the mouth of God."** *Mt 4:4*

The artwork of Dürer gives us an opportunity to pause and reflect. Although these images may only be a distant reflection of what actually occurred, nevertheless, the wounds were real. The precious blood was poured out, nails were driven into His hands, His heart was pierced for our sins and those of the whole world.

The reader may be moved but never quite satiated after reading these sacred pages. There is always more to ponder on His passion. We can meditate on these images until they touch and shape our minds and mold our hearts. We may never pray the same again. Like St. Augustine, we will remain restless until we come to the point in our lives that we trust Jesus unconditionally. This grace is ours because of what He has already accomplished for us through His passion, death and resurrection.

Brother Leonard Konopka, M.I.C.
Congregation of Marians of the Immaculate Conception

His Sorrowful Passion

Scriptural Chaplets of Divine Mercy

How to Pray the Chaplet of Divine Mercy

The Lord Jesus Christ taught St. Maria Faustina how to pray the Chaplet of Divine Mercy.

This prayer will serve to appease My wrath. You will recite it for nine days, on the beads of the rosary, in the following manner: First of all, you will say one OUR FATHER and HAIL MARY and the I BELIEVE IN GOD. Then on the OUR FATHER beads you will say the following words: "Eternal Father, I offer You the Body and Blood, Soul and Divinity of Your dearly beloved Son, Our Lord Jesus Christ, in atonement for our sins and those of the whole world." On the HAIL MARY beads you will say the following words: "For the sake of His sorrowful Passion, have mercy on us and on the whole world." In conclusion, three times you will recite these words. "Holy God, Holy Mighty One, Holy Immortal One, have mercy on us and on the whole world." *(Diary, 476)*

A Scriptural Chaplet of Divine Mercy
According to the Passion of Jesus Christ

Our Father, Who art in Heaven, hallowed be Thy Name. Thy kingdom come; Thy will be done on earth as it is in Heaven.

Give us this day our daily bread, and forgive us our trespasses, as we forgive those who trespass against us. And lead us not into temptation, but deliver us from evil. Amen.

Hail Mary, full of grace, the Lord is with thee; blessed art thou among women, and blessed is the Fruit of thy womb, Jesus.

Holy Mary, Mother of God, pray for us sinners, now and at the hour of our death. Amen.

I believe in God, the Father almighty, Creator of heaven and earth, and in Jesus Christ, his only Son, our Lord, who was conceived by the Holy Spirit, born of the Virgin Mary, suffered under Pontius Pilate, was crucified, died and was buried; he descended into hell; on the third day he rose again from the dead; he ascended into heaven, and is seated at the right hand of God the Father almighty; from there he will come to judge the living and the dead.

I believe in the Holy Spirit, the holy catholic Church, the communion of saints, the forgiveness of sins, the resurrection of the body, and life everlasting. Amen.

The Last Supper

The supper is ended. Let us go to Gethsemane.
Love is satisfied, And there the traitor is waiting. *(Diary, 1002)*

Eternal Father,
I offer You the Body and Blood, Soul and Divinity
of Your dearly beloved Son, Our Lord Jesus Christ,
in atonement for our sins and those of the whole world.

ave mercy on me, O God, have mercy on me: for my soul trusteth in thee. ... **Why do you trouble this woman? ... she hath done what she could: She is come beforehand to anoint my body for the burial.** *Ps 56:2, Mt 26:10, Mk 14:8*

For the sake of His sorrowful Passion,
have mercy on us and on the whole world.

e that dippeth his hand with me in the dish, he shall betray me. ... Take ye, and eat. This is my body. ... This is my blood of the [covenant], which shall be shed for many unto remission of sins. ... Jesus said to him: Judas, dost thou betray the Son of man with a kiss?
Mt 26:23,26,28, Lk 22:48

For the sake of His sorrowful Passion,
have mercy on us and on the whole world.

y soul is sorrowful even unto death: stay you here, and watch with me ... Could you not watch one hour with me? Watch ye, and pray. ... The sorrows of death have compassed me ... The Lord is merciful and just, and our God sheweth mercy. *Mt 26:38,40-41, Ps 114:3,5*

For the sake of His sorrowful Passion,
have mercy on us and on the whole world.

Christ on the Mount of Olives

Faithful submission to the will of God, always and everywhere, in all events and circumstances of life, gives great glory to God. *(Diary, 724)*

neeling down, he prayed ... **Abba, Father, all things are possible to thee: remove this chalice from me; but not what I will but what thou wilt.** ... Blessed be the God and Father of our Lord Jesus Christ, the Father of mercies, and the God of all comfort. *Lk 22:41, Mk 14:36, 2 Cor 1:3*

For the sake of His sorrowful Passion,
have mercy on us and on the whole world.

nd being in an agony, he prayed the longer. And his sweat became as drops of blood, trickling down upon the ground. ... And my soul is troubled exceedingly: but thou, O Lord, how long? Turn to me, O Lord, and deliver my soul: O save me for thy mercy's sake. *Lk 22:43-44, Ps 6:4-5*

For the sake of His sorrowful Passion,
have mercy on us and on the whole world.

eter remembered the word of Jesus which he had said: **Before the cock crow, thou wilt deny me thrice.** And going forth he wept bitterly. ... Out of the depths I have cried to thee, O Lord ... For with thee there is merciful forgiveness ... with the Lord there is mercy. *Mt 26:75, Ps 129:1,4,7*

For the sake of His sorrowful Passion,
have mercy on us and on the whole world.

Christ taken captive

Every grace gives the soul power and strength to act, and courage to suffer. The soul knows very well what God is asking of it, and it carries out His holy will despite adversities. *(Diary, 772)*

e hath borne the sins of many, and hath prayed for the transgressors. ... Thou shalt arise and have mercy on Sion: for it is time to have mercy on it, for the time is come. ... [A band of soldiers] and the tribune, and the servants of the Jews, took Jesus, and bound him. *Is 53:12, Ps 101:14, Jn 18:12*

For the sake of His sorrowful Passion,
have mercy on us and on the whole world.

rt thou the Christ the Son of the blessed God? And Jesus said to him: **I am.** ... Grace be with you, mercy, and peace from God the Father, and from Christ Jesus the Son of the Father; in truth and charity. ... Indeed this was the Son of God. *Mk 14:61-62, 2Jn 3, Mt 27:54*

For the sake of His sorrowful Passion,
have mercy on us and on the whole world.

he chief priests and the whole council sought false witness against Jesus, that they might put him to death. ... For thy mercy is magnified even to the heavens: and thy truth unto the clouds. ... **Every one that is of the truth, heareth my voice.** Pilate saith to him: What is truth? *Mt 26:59, Ps 56:11, Jn 18:37-38*

For the sake of His sorrowful Passion,
have mercy on us and on the whole world.

e is guilty of death. Then they did spit in his face, and buffeted him: and others struck his face with the palms of their hands, Saying: Prophesy unto us, O Christ, who is he that struck thee? ... Have mercy on me, O God, for man hath trodden me under foot; all the day long he hath afflicted me fighting against me. *Mt 26:66-68, Ps 55:2*

For the sake of His sorrowful Passion,
have mercy on us and on the whole world.

Flagellation of Christ

There is more merit to one hour of meditation on My sorrowful Passion than there is to a whole year of flagellation that draws blood; the contemplation of My painful wounds is of great profit to you ... *(Diary, 369)*

Eternal Father,
I offer You the Body and Blood, Soul and Divinity
of Your dearly beloved Son, Our Lord Jesus Christ,
in atonement for our sins and those of the whole world.

For I am ready for scourges: and my sorrow is continually before me. ... But my enemies live, and are stronger than I: and they that hate me wrongfully are multiplied. ... For it will come to pass that Herod will seek the child to destroy him. *Ps 37:18,20, Mt 2:13*

For the sake of His sorrowful Passion,
have mercy on us and on the whole world.

The Pharisees going out, immediately made a consultation with the Herodians against him, how they might destroy him. ... Herod seeing Jesus, was very glad; for he was desirous of a long time to see him, because he had heard many things of him; and he hoped to see some sign wrought by him. *Mk 3:6, Lk 23:8*

For the sake of His sorrowful Passion,
have mercy on us and on the whole world.

All the chief priests and ancients of the people took counsel against Jesus, that they might put him to death. ... When he was accused by the chief priests and ancients, he answered nothing. *Mt 27:1,12*

For the sake of His sorrowful Passion,
have mercy on us and on the whole world.

He was offered because it was his own will, and he opened not his mouth: he shall be led as a sheep to the slaughter, and shall be dumb as a lamb before his shearer, and he shall not open his mouth. *Is 53:7*

For the sake of His sorrowful Passion,
have mercy on us and on the whole world.

They brought him bound, and delivered him to Pontius Pilate the governor. ... And the whole people answering, said: His blood be upon us and upon our children. ... And spitting upon him, they took the reed, and struck his head. *Mt 27:2,25,30*

For the sake of His sorrowful Passion,
have mercy on us and on the whole world.

And stripping him, they put a scarlet cloak about him ... **And to him that striketh thee on the one cheek, offer also the other. And him that taketh away from thee thy cloak, forbid not to take thy coat also.** *Mt 27:28, Lk 6:29*

For the sake of His sorrowful Passion,
have mercy on us and on the whole world.

For my iniquities are gone over my head: and as a heavy burden are become heavy upon me ... I am afflicted and humbled exceedingly: I roared with the groaning of my heart. *Ps 37:5,9*

For the sake of His sorrowful Passion,
have mercy on us and on the whole world.

Christ before the people

Encourage souls to place great trust in My fathomless mercy. Let the weak, sinful soul have no fear to approach Me, for even if it had more sins than there are grains of sand in the world, all would be drowned in the unmeasureable depth of My mercy. *(Diary, 1059)*

𝕻ilate took Jesus, and scourged him. ... I have given my body to the strikers, and my cheeks to them that plucked them: I have not turned away my face from them that rebuked me, and spit upon me. ... Blessed be the Lord my God ... My mercy, and my refuge: my support, and my deliverer. *Jn 19:1, Is 50:6, Ps 143:1-2*

> *For the sake of His sorrowful Passion,*
> *have mercy on us and on the whole world.*

𝕳e hath torn me with wound upon wound. ... Yet so, that [the stripes] exceed not the number of forty: lest thy brother depart shamefully torn before thy eyes. ... Out of the depths I have cried to thee, O Lord: Lord, hear my voice. ... For with thee there is merciful forgiveness. *Job 16:15, Dt 25:3, Ps 129:1-2,4*

> *For the sake of His sorrowful Passion,*
> *have mercy on us and on the whole world.*

𝕱or day and night thy hand was heavy upon me: I am turned in my anguish, whilst the thorn is fastened. ... Many are the scourges of the sinner, but mercy shall encompass him that hopeth in the Lord. *Ps 31:4,10*

> *For the sake of His sorrowful Passion,*
> *have mercy on us and on the whole world.*

Eternal Father,
I offer You the Body and Blood, Soul and Divinity
of Your dearly beloved Son, Our Lord Jesus Christ,
in atonement for our sins and those of the whole world.

A man of sorrows ... He hath borne our infirmities and carried our sorrows. ... He was wounded for our iniquities, he was bruised for our sins: the chastisement of our peace was upon him, and by his bruises we are healed. *Is 53:3-5*

For the sake of His sorrowful Passion,
have mercy on us and on the whole world.

J esus answered: **My kingdom is not of this world.** ... And the soldiers platting a crown of thorns, put it upon his head ... they gave him blows. *Jn 18:36, Jn 19:2-3*

For the sake of His sorrowful Passion,
have mercy on us and on the whole world.

H ow long do you rush in upon a man? you all kill, as if you were thrusting down a leaning wall, and a tottering fence. *Ps 61:4*

For the sake of His sorrowful Passion,
have mercy on us and on the whole world.

Have mercy on me, O God, for man hath trodden me under foot; all the day long he hath afflicted me fighting against me. ... I will not fear what flesh can do against me. *Ps 55:2,5*

For the sake of His sorrowful Passion,
have mercy on us and on the whole world.

For thou scourgest, and thou savest: thou leadest down to hell, and bringest up again: and there is none that can escape thy hand. *Tb 13:2*

For the sake of His sorrowful Passion,
have mercy on us and on the whole world.

And they began to salute him: Hail, king of the Jews. And they struck his head with a reed: and they did spit on him. And bowing their knees, they adored him. *Mk 15:18-19*

For the sake of His sorrowful Passion,
have mercy on us and on the whole world.

Crucify him, crucify him. ... We have no king but Caesar. ... The sorrows of death surrounded me. ... The sorrows of hell encompassed me. *Jn 19:6,15, Ps 17:5-6*

For the sake of His sorrowful Passion,
have mercy on us and on the whole world.

Christ bearing the Cross

From all My wounds, like from streams, mercy flows for souls, but the wound in My Heart is the fountain of unfathomable mercy. *(Diary, 1190)*

ause me to hear thy mercy in the morning; for in thee I have hoped. Make the way known to me, wherein I should walk. ... And bearing his own cross, he went forth to ... Golgotha. ... **If any man will come after me, let him deny himself, and take up his cross, and follow me.** *Ps 142:8, Jn 19:17, Mt 16:24*

For the sake of His sorrowful Passion,
have mercy on us and on the whole world.

can do all things in him who strengtheneth me. ... And going out, they found a man of Cyrene, named Simon: him they forced to take up his cross. *Phil 4:13, Mt 27:32*

For the sake of His sorrowful Passion,
have mercy on us and on the whole world.

nd there followed him a great multitude of people, and of women, who bewailed and lamented him. But Jesus turning to them, said: **Daughters of Jerusalem, weep not over me; but weep for yourselves, and for your children.** *Lk 23:27-28*

For the sake of His sorrowful Passion,
have mercy on us and on the whole world.

Eternal Father,
I offer You the Body and Blood, Soul and Divinity
of Your dearly beloved Son, Our Lord Jesus Christ,
in atonement for our sins and those of the whole world.

When they were come to the place which is called Calvary, they crucified him there; and the robbers, one on the right hand, and the other on the left. *Lk 23:33*

For the sake of His sorrowful Passion,
have mercy on us and on the whole world.

Jesus said: **Father, forgive them, for they know not what they do.** But they, dividing his garments, cast lots. *Lk 23:34*

For the sake of His sorrowful Passion,
have mercy on us and on the whole world.

And to him that striketh thee on the one cheek, offer also the other. And him that taketh away from thee thy cloak, forbid not to take thy coat also.** *Lk 6:29*

For the sake of His sorrowful Passion,
have mercy on us and on the whole world.

Thou hast mercy upon all, because thou canst do all things, and overlookest the sins of men for the sake of repentance. *Wis 11:24*

For the sake of His sorrowful Passion,
have mercy on us and on the whole world.

The Crucifixion

Jesus said to St. Maria Faustina: **At three o'clock, implore My mercy, especially for sinners; and, if only for a brief moment, immerse yourself in My Passion ... This is the hour of great mercy for the whole world.** *(Diary, 1320)*

He saved others; himself he cannot save. Let Christ the king of Israel come down now from the cross, that we may see and believe. *Mk 15:31-32*

For the sake of His sorrowful Passion,
have mercy on us and on the whole world.

They that were crucified with him reviled him. ... For what is my strength, that I can hold out? ... My strength is not the strength of stones, nor is my flesh of brass. *Mk 15:32, Job 6:11-12*

For the sake of His sorrowful Passion,
have mercy on us and on the whole world.

O God, be merciful to me a sinner ... Neither dost thou fear God, seeing thou art under the same condemnation? And we indeed justly, for we receive the due reward of our deeds; but this man hath done no evil. *Lk 18:13, Lk 23:40-41*

For the sake of His sorrowful Passion,
have mercy on us and on the whole world.

He that shall confess, and forsake [his sins], shall obtain mercy. ... He said to Jesus: Lord, remember me when thou shalt come into thy kingdom. And Jesus said to him: **Amen I say to thee, this day thou shalt be with me in paradise.** *Prv 28:13, Lk 23:42-43*

For the sake of His sorrowful Passion,
have mercy on us and on the whole world.

Behold the Lamb of God, behold him who taketh away the sin of the world ... a lamb without blemish—sacrifice[d] in the evening. ... When the sixth hour was come, there was darkness over the whole earth until the ninth hour. *Jn 1:29, Ex 12:5-6, Mk 15:33*

For the sake of His sorrowful Passion,
have mercy on us and on the whole world.

Jesus cried out with a loud voice, saying: **Eloi, Eloi, lamma sabacthani? ... My God, my God, why hast thou forsaken me?** ... I am a worm, and no man: the reproach of men, and the outcast of the people. *Mk 15:34, Ps 21:7*

For the sake of His sorrowful Passion,
have mercy on us and on the whole world.

Eternal Father,
I offer You the Body and Blood, Soul and Divinity
of Your dearly beloved Son, Our Lord Jesus Christ,
in atonement for our sins and those of the whole world.

Now there stood by the cross of Jesus, his mother, and his mother's sister, Mary of Cleophas, and Mary Magdalen. *Jn 19:25*

For the sake of His sorrowful Passion,
have mercy on us and on the whole world.

When Jesus therefore had seen his mother and the disciple standing whom he loved, he saith, to his mother: **Woman, behold thy son.** *Jn 19:26*

For the sake of His sorrowful Passion,
have mercy on us and on the whole world.

See if there be any sorrow like to my sorrow. ... Son, ... I have sought thee sorrowing. ... He saith to the disciple: **Behold thy mother.** *Lam 1:12, Lk 2:48, Jn 19:27*

For the sake of His sorrowful Passion,
have mercy on us and on the whole world.

The Lamentation for Christ

You expired, Jesus, but the source of life gushed forth for souls, and the ocean of mercy opened up for the whole world. *(Diary, 1319)*

Thou, O Lord, art a God of compassion, and merciful, patient, and of much mercy ... have mercy on me: give thy command to thy servant, and save the son of thy handmaid. *Ps 85:15-16*

For the sake of His sorrowful Passion,
have mercy on us and on the whole world.

Have mercy on me, O Lord, for I am weak: heal me, O Lord, for my bones are troubled. ... **I thirst** ... They, putting a sponge full of vinegar about hyssop, put it to his mouth. *Ps 6:3, Jn 19:28-29*

For the sake of His sorrowful Passion,
have mercy on us and on the whole world.

Have mercy on me, O God, according to thy great mercy. ... Jesus therefore, when he had taken the vinegar, said: **It is consummated.** *Ps 50:3, Jn 19:30*

For the sake of His sorrowful Passion,
have mercy on us and on the whole world.

And Jesus crying with a loud voice, said: **Father, into thy hands I commend my spirit.** And saying this, he gave up the ghost. *Lk 23:46*

For the sake of His sorrowful Passion,
have mercy on us and on the whole world.

The Entombment

The Lord's Promise: **The souls that say this chaplet will be embraced by My mercy during their lifetime and especially at the hour of their death.** *(Diary, 754)*

Behold this child is set for the fall, and for the resurrection of many in Israel, and for a sign which shall be contradicted; And thy own soul a sword shall pierce. *Lk 2:34-35*

> *For the sake of His sorrowful Passion,*
> *have mercy on us and on the whole world.*

They shall look upon me, whom they have pierced: and they shall mourn for him as one mourneth for an only son ... to grieve for the death of the firstborn. ... One of the soldiers with a spear opened his side, and immediately there came out blood and water. *Zac 12:10, Jn 19:34*

> *For the sake of His sorrowful Passion,*
> *have mercy on us and on the whole world.*

Bless the Lord, O my soul, and never forget all he hath done for thee. ... Who redeemeth thy life from destruction: who crowneth thee with mercy and compassion. ... And taking him down, he wrapped him in fine linen, and laid him in a sepulchre ... [The women] prepared spices and ointments. *Ps 102:2,4, Lk 23:53,56*

> *For the sake of His sorrowful Passion,*
> *have mercy on us and on the whole world.*

The Resurrection of Christ

Eternal Truth, give me a ray of Your light that I may come to know You, O Lord, and worthily glorify Your infinite mercy. *(Diary, 727)*

*Holy God, Holy Mighty One, Holy Immortal One,
have mercy on us and on the whole world.*

*Holy God, Holy Mighty One, Holy Immortal One,
have mercy on us and on the whole world.*

*Holy God, Holy Mighty One, Holy Immortal One,
have mercy on us and on the whole world.*

Concluding Prayer (Optional)

Eternal God, in whom mercy is endless and the treasury of compassion inexhaustible, look kindly upon us and increase Your mercy in us, that in difficult moments we might not despair nor become despondent, but with great confidence submit ourselves to Your holy will, which is Love and Mercy itself. (Diary, 950)

The Divine Mercy Novena

Jesus, I trust in You.

Novena to The Divine Mercy which Jesus instructed me to write down and make before the Feast of Mercy. It begins on Good Friday. **I desire that during these nine days you bring souls to the fountain of My mercy, that they may draw therefrom strength and refreshment and whatever grace they need in the hardships of life, and especially at the hour of death. On each day you will bring to My Heart a different group of souls, and you will immerse them in this ocean of My mercy, and I will bring all these souls into the house of My Father.** *(Diary 1209)*

First Day

Today, bring to Me all mankind, especially all sinners, and immerse them in the ocean of My mercy. In this way you will console Me in the bitter grief into which the loss of souls plunges Me. *(Diary 1210)*

Second Day

Today bring to me the souls of priests and religious, and immerse them in My unfathomable mercy. It was they who gave Me the strength to endure My bitter Passion. Through them, as through channels, My mercy flows out upon mankind. *(Diary 1212)*

Third Day

Today bring to Me all devout and faithful souls, and immerse them in the ocean of My mercy. These souls brought Me consolation on the Way of the Cross. They were that drop of consolation in the midst of an ocean of bitterness. *(Diary, 1214)*

Fourth Day

Today bring to Me the pagans and those who do not yet know Me. I was thinking also of them during My bitter Passion, and their future zeal comforted My Heart. Immerse them in the ocean of My mercy. *(Diary, 1216)*

Fifth Day

Today bring to Me the souls of heretics and schismatics, and immerse them in the ocean of My mercy. During My bitter Passion they tore at My Body and Heart; that is, My Church. As they return to unity with the Church, My wounds heal, and in this way they alleviate My Passion. *(Diary, 1218)*

Sixth Day

Today bring to me the meek and humble souls and the souls of little children, and immerse them in My mercy. These souls most closely resemble My Heart. They strengthened Me during My bitter agony. I saw them as earthly Angels, who would keep vigil at My altars. I pour out upon them whole torrents of grace. Only the humble soul is able to receive My grace. I favor humble souls with My confidence. *(Diary,1220)*

Seventh Day

Today bring to me the souls who especially venerate and glorify My mercy, and immerse them in My mercy. These souls sorrowed most over My Passion and entered most deeply into My Spirit. They are living images of My Compassionate heart. These souls will shine with a special brightness in the next life. Not one of them will go into the fire of hell. I shall particularly defend each one of them at the hour of death. *(Diary, 1224)*

Eighth Day

Today bring to Me the souls who are in the prison of Purgatory, and immerse them in the abyss of My mercy. Let the torrents of My Blood cool down their scorching flames. All these souls are greatly loved by Me. They are making retribution to My justice. It is in your power to bring them relief. Draw all the indulgences from the treasury of My Church and offer them on their behalf. Oh, if you only knew the torments they suffer, you would continually offer for them the alms of the spirit and pay off their debt to My justice. *(Diary, 1226)*

Ninth Day

Today bring to Me souls who have become lukewarm, and immerse them in the abyss of My mercy. These souls wound My Heart most painfully. My soul suffered the most dreadful loathing in the Garden of Olives because of lukewarm souls. They were the reason I cried out: "Father, take this cup away from Me, if it be Your will." For them, the last hope of salvation is to flee to My mercy. *(Diary, 1228)*

A Scriptural Chaplet of Divine Mercy:

Meditations from the Seven Penitential Psalms

Ps 6, Ps 31(32), Ps 37(38), Ps 50(51), Ps 101(102),
Ps 129(130), and Ps 142(143)

Our Father, Who art in Heaven, hallowed be Thy Name. Thy kingdom come; Thy will be done on earth as it is in Heaven.

Give us this day our daily bread, and forgive us our trespasses, as we forgive those who trespass against us. And lead us not into temptation, but deliver us from evil. Amen.

Hail Mary, full of grace, the Lord is with thee; blessed art thou among women, and blessed is the Fruit of thy womb, Jesus.

Holy Mary, Mother of God, pray for us sinners, now and at the hour of our death. Amen.

I believe in God, the Father almighty, Creator of heaven and earth, and in Jesus Christ, his only Son, our Lord, who was conceived by the Holy Spirit, born of the Virgin Mary, suffered under Pontius Pilate, was crucified, died and was buried; he descended into hell; on the third day he rose again from the dead; he ascended into heaven, and is seated at the right hand of God the Father almighty; from there he will come to judge the living and the dead.

I believe in the Holy Spirit, the holy catholic Church, the communion of saints, the forgiveness of sins, the resurrection of the body, and life everlasting. Amen.

Eternal Father,
I offer You the Body and Blood, Soul and Divinity
of Your dearly beloved Son, Our Lord Jesus Christ,
in atonement for our sins and those of the whole world.

O LORD, rebuke me not in thy indignation, nor chastise me in thy wrath. *Ps 6:2*

> *For the sake of His sorrowful Passion,*
> *have mercy on us and on the whole world.*

Have mercy on me, O Lord, for I am weak: heal me, O Lord, for my bones are troubled. *Ps 6:3*

> *For the sake of His sorrowful Passion,*
> *have mercy on us and on the whole world.*

And my soul is troubled exceedingly: but thou, O Lord, how long? *Ps 6:4*

> *For the sake of His sorrowful Passion,*
> *have mercy on us and on the whole world.*

Turn to me, O Lord, and deliver my soul: O save me for thy mercy's sake. ... who shall confess to thee in hell? *Ps 6:5-6*

> *For the sake of His sorrowful Passion,*
> *have mercy on us and on the whole world.*

I have laboured in my groanings, every night I will wash my bed: I will water my couch with my tears. *Ps 6:7*

> *For the sake of His sorrowful Passion,*
> *have mercy on us and on the whole world.*

Depart from me, all ye workers of iniquity: for the Lord hath heard the voice of my weeping. *Ps 6:9*

For the sake of His sorrowful Passion,
have mercy on us and on the whole world.

The Lord hath heard my supplication: the Lord hath received my prayer. *Ps 6:10*

For the sake of His sorrowful Passion,
have mercy on us and on the whole world.

Blessed are they whose iniquities are forgiven, and whose sins are covered. *Ps 31:1*

For the sake of His sorrowful Passion,
have mercy on us and on the whole world.

For day and night thy hand was heavy upon me: I am turned in my anguish, whilst the thorn is fastened. *Ps 31:4*

For the sake of His sorrowful Passion,
have mercy on us and on the whole world.

Thou art my refuge from the trouble which hath encompassed me: my joy, deliver me from them that surround me. *Ps 31:7*

For the sake of His sorrowful Passion,
have mercy on us and on the whole world.

Eternal Father,
I offer You the Body and Blood, Soul and Divinity
of Your dearly beloved Son, Our Lord Jesus Christ,
in atonement for our sins and those of the whole world.

I will give thee understanding, and I will instruct thee in this way, in which thou shalt go: I will fix my eyes upon thee. *Ps 31:8*

> *For the sake of His sorrowful Passion,*
> *have mercy on us and on the whole world.*

Many are the scourges of the sinner, but mercy shall encompass him that hopeth in the Lord. *Ps 31:10*

> *For the sake of His sorrowful Passion,*
> *have mercy on us and on the whole world.*

Be glad in the Lord, and rejoice, ye just, and glory, all ye right of heart. *Ps 31:11*

> *For the sake of His sorrowful Passion,*
> *have mercy on us and on the whole world.*

Rebuke me not, O Lord, in thy indignation ... For thy arrows are fastened in me: and thy hand hath been strong upon me. *Ps 37:2-3*

> *For the sake of His sorrowful Passion,*
> *have mercy on us and on the whole world.*

There is no health in my flesh, because of thy wrath: there is no peace for my bones, because of my sins. *Ps 37:4*

> *For the sake of His sorrowful Passion,*
> *have mercy on us and on the whole world.*

I am become miserable, and am bowed down even to the end: I walked sorrowful all the day long. *Ps 37:7*

> *For the sake of His sorrowful Passion,*
> *have mercy on us and on the whole world.*

I am afflicted and humbled exceedingly: I roared with the groaning of my heart. *Ps 37:9*

> *For the sake of His sorrowful Passion,*
> *have mercy on us and on the whole world.*

Lord, all my desire is before thee, and my groaning is not hidden from thee. My heart is troubled, my strength hath left me. *Ps 37:10-11*

> *For the sake of His sorrowful Passion,*
> *have mercy on us and on the whole world.*

My friends and my neighbours have drawn near, and stood against me. And they that were near me stood afar off: And they that sought my soul used violence. *Ps 37:12-13*

> *For the sake of His sorrowful Passion,*
> *have mercy on us and on the whole world.*

For in thee, O Lord, have I hoped: thou wilt hear me, O Lord my God. *Ps 37:16*

> *For the sake of His sorrowful Passion,*
> *have mercy on us and on the whole world.*

Eternal Father,
I offer You the Body and Blood, Soul and Divinity
of Your dearly beloved Son, Our Lord Jesus Christ,
in atonement for our sins and those of the whole world.

For I am ready for scourges: and my sorrow is continually before me. *Ps 37:18*

For the sake of His sorrowful Passion,
have mercy on us and on the whole world.

Forsake me not, O Lord my God: do not thou depart from me. Attend unto my help, O Lord, the God of my salvation. *Ps 37:22-23*

For the sake of His sorrowful Passion,
have mercy on us and on the whole world.

Have mercy on me, O God, according to thy great mercy. And according to the multitude of thy tender mercies blot out my iniquity. ... Thou shalt wash me, and I shall be made whiter than snow. *Ps 50:3,9*

For the sake of His sorrowful Passion,
have mercy on us and on the whole world.

To my hearing thou shalt give joy and gladness: and the bones that have been humbled shall rejoice. Turn away thy face from my sins, and blot out all my iniquities. *Ps 50:10-11*

For the sake of His sorrowful Passion,
have mercy on us and on the whole world

Create a clean heart in me, O God. ... Cast me not away from thy face; and take not thy holy spirit from me. *Ps 50:12-13*

> *For the sake of His sorrowful Passion,*
> *have mercy on us and on the whole world.*

Restore unto me the joy of thy salvation, and strengthen me with a perfect spirit. *Ps 50:14*

> *For the sake of His sorrowful Passion,*
> *have mercy on us and on the whole world.*

A sacrifice to God is an afflicted spirit: a contrite and humbled heart, O God, thou wilt not despise. *Ps 50:19*

> *For the sake of His sorrowful Passion,*
> *have mercy on us and on the whole world.*

Hear, O Lord, my prayer: and let my cry come to thee. *Ps 101:2*

> *For the sake of His sorrowful Passion,*
> *have mercy on us and on the whole world.*

Turn not away thy face from me: in the day when I am in trouble, incline thy ear to me. In what day soever I shall call upon thee, hear me speedily. *Ps 101:3*

> *For the sake of His sorrowful Passion,*
> *have mercy on us and on the whole world.*

All the day long my enemies reproached me: and they that praised me did swear against me. *Ps 101:9*

> *For the sake of His sorrowful Passion,*
> *have mercy on us and on the whole world.*

Eternal Father,
I offer You the Body and Blood, Soul and Divinity
of Your dearly beloved Son, Our Lord Jesus Christ,
in atonement for our sins and those of the whole world.

Thou shalt arise and have mercy on Sion: for it is time to have mercy on it, for the time is come. *Ps 101:14*

For the sake of His sorrowful Passion,
have mercy on us and on the whole world.

For the Lord hath built up Sion: and he shall be seen in his glory. *Ps 101:17*

For the sake of His sorrowful Passion,
have mercy on us and on the whole world.

He hath had regard to the prayer of the humble: and he hath not despised their petition. *Ps 101:18*

For the sake of His sorrowful Passion,
have mercy on us and on the whole world.

Out of the depths I have cried to thee, O Lord. *Ps 129:1*

For the sake of His sorrowful Passion,
have mercy on us and on the whole world.

Lord, hear my voice. Let thy ears be attentive to the voice of my supplication. *Ps 129:2*

For the sake of His sorrowful Passion,
have mercy on us and on the whole world.

For with thee there is merciful forgiveness: and by reason of thy law, I have waited for thee, O Lord. *Ps 129:4*

For the sake of His sorrowful Passion,
have mercy on us and on the whole world.

My soul hath relied on his word: my soul hath hoped in the Lord. *Ps 129:4-5*

For the sake of His sorrowful Passion,
have mercy on us and on the whole world.

From the morning watch even until night, let Israel hope in the Lord. *Ps 129:6*

For the sake of His sorrowful Passion,
have mercy on us and on the whole world.

Because with the Lord there is mercy: and with him plentiful redemption. *Ps 129:7*

For the sake of His sorrowful Passion,
have mercy on us and on the whole world.

And he shall redeem Israel from all his iniquities. *Ps 129:8*

For the sake of His sorrowful Passion,
have mercy on us and on the whole world.

Eternal Father,
I offer You the Body and Blood, Soul and Divinity
of Your dearly beloved Son, Our Lord Jesus Christ,
in atonement for our sins and those of the whole world.

Hear, O Lord, my prayer: give ear to my supplication in thy truth: hear me in thy justice. *Ps 142:1*

> *For the sake of His sorrowful Passion,*
> *have mercy on us and on the whole world.*

For the enemy hath persecuted my soul: he hath brought down my life to the earth. *Ps 142:3*

> *For the sake of His sorrowful Passion,*
> *have mercy on us and on the whole world.*

He hath made me to dwell in darkness as those that have been dead of old: and my spirit is in anguish within me: my heart within me is troubled. *Ps 142:3-4*

> *For the sake of His sorrowful Passion,*
> *have mercy on us and on the whole world.*

I stretched forth my hands to thee: my soul is as earth without water unto thee. *Ps 142:6*

> *For the sake of His sorrowful Passion,*
> *have mercy on us and on the whole world.*

Hear me, speedily, O Lord: my spirit hath fainted away. Turn not away thy face from me. *Ps 142:7*

> *For the sake of His sorrowful Passion,*
> *have mercy on us and on the whole world.*

Cause me to hear thy mercy in the morning; for in thee have I hoped. *Ps 142:8*

> *For the sake of His sorrowful Passion,*
> *have mercy on us and on the whole world.*

Make the way known to me, wherein I should walk: for I have lifted up my soul to thee. *Ps 142:8*

> *For the sake of His sorrowful Passion,*
> *have mercy on us and on the whole world.*

Deliver me from my enemies, O Lord, to thee have I fled: teach me to do thy will, for thou art my God. *Ps 142:9-10*

> *For the sake of His sorrowful Passion,*
> *have mercy on us and on the whole world.*

Thou wilt bring my soul out of trouble: and in thy mercy thou wilt destroy my enemies. *Ps 142:11-12*

> *For the sake of His sorrowful Passion,*
> *have mercy on us and on the whole world.*

I am thy servant. *Ps 142:12*

> *For the sake of His sorrowful Passion*
> *have mercy on us and on the whole world.*

*Holy God, Holy Mighty One, Holy Immortal One,
have mercy on us and on the whole world.*

*Holy God, Holy Mighty One, Holy Immortal One,
have mercy on us and on the whole world.*

*Holy God, Holy Mighty One, Holy Immortal One,
have mercy on us and on the whole world.*

Concluding Prayer (Optional)

Eternal God, in whom mercy is endless and the treasury of compassion inexhaustible, look kindly upon us and increase Your mercy in us, that in difficult moments we might not despair nor become despondent, but with great confidence submit ourselves to Your holy will, which is Love and Mercy itself. (Diary, 950)

Author's Note

Several years ago, I shared with a priest a Scriptural Rosary I wrote on the Virtue of Justice. He said, "Do not put Justice in isolation. Justice and Mercy are two blades of the same sword. They compliment each other." Then, I proceeded to write a Scriptural Rosary highlighting the message of God's Mercy as seen in the fifteen mysteries of the Most Holy Rosary. The struggle to write this Scriptural Rosary was like being lost in a maze of caves and in every direction I turned I wandered down another dead end. I spent countless hours praying, searching, writing, rewriting, researching and praying, but to no avail. I always found myself down another dead end.

During this period of struggle, Father Vincent P. Bork and Nancy Scimone Bash of Saint Gabriel Media introduced me to the Chaplet of Divine Mercy. At that time we were collaborating on The Sanctity of Life Scriptural Rosary recording project. Since then, I have listened to Nancy's marvelous recording of the Chaplet of Divine Mercy for many hours, primarily while commuting. However, I never fully immersed myself in the devotion, because I felt that this particular devotion would somehow take me away from my devotion to the Most Holy Rosary. My blinded, limited thinking forced me to believe I could only pray the Chaplet of Divine Mercy or the Most Holy Rosary, but not both. This was a silly, spiritually immature idea.

Laboring endlessly on the Mercy Scriptural Rosary, I was getting nowhere. Then, I turned to St. Maria Faustina, the Apostle of Divine Mercy, for help. In the 1930s, Saint Maria Faustina received from the Lord a message of mercy and began keeping a diary at the request of her spiritual director and Jesus. Her diary records four years of divine revelations and mystical experiences concerning God's mercy. She was canonized in the Jubilee Year, 2000. I read her diary, <u>Divine Mercy in My Soul</u>, for insight on God's Mercy. She turned on the light in the cave and I was no longer blinded by my previous limited thinking. It was not a Scriptural Rosary of Mercy that I should write but a Scriptural Chaplet of Divine Mercy.

St. Maria Faustina taught me the genius of praying. We can pray both the Chaplet of Divine Mercy and the Most Holy Rosary, because all different methods of prayer bring us closer to knowing Jesus Christ and His Blessed Mother.

An integral part of the Most Holy Rosary is meditation on the Joyful, Sorrowful, and Glorious mysteries. If we avoid meditating on the mysteries during prayer, we can be admonished as "babbling like the pagans." If we do not focus on Jesus' Passion, we can struggle with the repetition of the prayers of the Chaplet of Divine Mercy. Jesus spoke of meditation to St. Maria Faustina, when He said: **My daughter, meditate frequently on the sufferings which I have undergone for your sake, and then nothing of what you suffer for Me will seem great to you. You please Me most when you meditate on My Sorrowful Passion. Join your little sufferings to My Sorrowful Passion, so that they may have infinite value before My Majesty.** *(Diary, 1512).* When we find ourselves struggling with mental prayer we can turn to Sacred Scriptures and through God's Word we can find the images and descriptions that allow us to call to mind the events of Jesus' Passion and thus we can meditate more intently.

This book features two Scriptural Chaplets of Divine Mercy that can help us meditate. The first Scriptural Chaplet chronicles Jesus' Passion and has Scripture selections from:

• The Chronology of the Passion from the Gospels of St. Matthew, St. Mark, St. Luke and St. John.

• The Seven Last Words of Jesus on the Cross.

• Selections from The Suffering Servant's Songs of Isaiah. *(Is 42:1-4; 49:1-7; 50:4-11; 52:13-15,53)*

• Mary's Seven Sorrows. (Simeon's prophecy that a sword of sorrow would pierce her heart, fleeing into Egypt to escape King Herod, searching for the child Jesus for three days and then finding of Jesus in the temple, meeting Jesus during the carrying of the cross, standing at the foot of the cross during the Crucifixion, holding of the body of Jesus following the removal from the cross, and assisting in the burial of Jesus)

Albrecht Dürer's 15th century woodcut illustrations from **The Great Passion** series illustrate this Scriptural Chaplet.

The second Scriptural Chaplet of Divine Mercy is based on the seven Psalms, [Ps 6, Ps 31(32), Ps 37(38), Ps 50(51), Ps 101(102), Ps 129(130), and Ps 142(143)], called the Penitential Psalms by the 6th century monk Cassiodorus. Through their recitation, we increase our awareness of sin, express deep sorrow and repentance for sin, and recognize how to pray and hope for pardon and forgiveness through God's mercy. Ten days prior to St. Augustine's death on August 28th, 430, he had these seven Psalms written on the walls around his deathbed and in seclusion he continually prayed these psalms and wept tears of repentance at the final hours of his death. By combining meditations from the Penitential Psalms with the prayers of the Chaplet of Divine Mercy, we can hope in Jesus' promise: **I have opened My heart as a living fountain of mercy. Let all souls draw life from it. Let them approach this sea of mercy with great trust. ... whoever places his trust in My mercy will be filled with My divine peace at the hour of death.** *(Diary, 1520)*

In my previous Scriptural prayer books, I refer to the New American Bible translation for my meditation selections. However, for this book I selected the Douay-Rheims Bible for the Sacred Scriptures references since it translates Hell as Hell, not as the lower regions or bowels of the earth or the nether world. In her Diary, St. Maria Faustina wrote that she was led by an angel to the chasms of Hell: "I am writing this at the command of God, so that no soul may find an excuse by saying there is no hell, or that nobody has ever been there, and so no one can say what it is like. I, Sister Faustina, by the order of God, have visited the abysses of hell so that I might tell souls about it and testify to its existence." *(Diary, 741)*

May God bless you and may His Divine Mercy shine on you, yours and the whole world.

Christine Haapala

Christ in Limbo

I, Sister Faustina, by the order of God, have visited the abysses of hell so that I might tell souls about it and testify to its existence. ... most of the souls there are those who disbelieved that there is a hell. *(Diary, 741)*

The Dürer Gothic Condensed Capital Letters

𝕬 𝕭 𝕮 𝕯 𝕰 𝕱

𝕲 𝕳 𝕴 𝕵 𝕶 𝕷

𝕸 𝕹 𝕺 𝕻 𝕼

𝕽 𝕾 𝕿 𝖀 𝖁

𝖂 𝖃 𝖄 𝖅

Other Works by Christine Haapala

Prayer Books for Children

Speak, Lord, I am Listening *A Scriptural Rosary Book*

Follow Me *A Scriptural Stations of the Cross Book*

Prayer Books for Teens and Adults

The Psalter of Jesus and Mary *A Scriptural Rosary according to Psalms and Proverbs*

Pearls of Peace *A Rosary Journey through the Holy Land*

The Suffering Servant's Courage *A Scriptural Rosary Book*

From Genesis to Revelation *Seven Scriptural Rosaries*

Seraphim and Cherubim *A Scriptural Chaplet of the Holy Angels*

In His Presence *Seven Visits to the Blessed Sacrament*

Sanctify my Heart *A Scriptural Novena to the Holy Spirit*

Prayer CDs

The Sanctity of Life *Scriptural Rosary*

Time for Mercy *A Scriptural Chaplet of Divine Mercy*

Ordering Information

To purchase additional copies of this book or the other works mentioned above, please visit your local Catholic bookstore or visit us on-line at www.sufferingservant.com.